PUZZLE JOURNEY
AROUND
THE WORLD

Lesley Sims
Illustrated by Sue Stitt

Designed by Lucy Parris
Edited by Jenny Tyler
Series Editor: Gaby Waters

Eli   Su

Here are Eli, Su and Em. They are out shopping
She keeps stopping to chat and they're fe
Little do they know that an exciting adven
to happen. Turn the page and share it with them.

The junk shop

"Meet you back here in twenty minutes!" Aunt Rose had said and disappeared.

So Em, Su and Eli were left in the hot, stuffy mall, waiting for her.

"This is boring," said Em. "Let's go for a walk."

They wandered outside. Before long, they were in a part of town they hadn't visited before.

There were other stores to look at, but it still wasn't much fun. Then Eli found one that looked different.

"Let's go in here," he called to the other two, as he opened the door. A bell jangled noisily.

Inside, they found the oddest collection of things. Eli picked up a globe half-heartedly. All at once, he had a strange feeling that he had to buy it.

"You really want that old thing?" the lady asked him. Eli nodded. "There's a bag to go with it somewhere," she said, describing it.

"They have to be sold together. Don't ask me why!" She looked around, but she couldn't find it.

Can you find the bag?

3

Egbert the explorer?

"I'm afraid the globe and bag are very battered," the lady told Eli. "They belonged to my great-grandfather Egbert." She pointed to a painting.

"That's him. He always wanted to be an explorer. Instead, he had to work in a bank." She smiled. "So he spent all his time daydreaming."

"He pretended he'd been all over the world. He lived in a world of his own more like. Well, enjoy your geography lessons," she laughed, as Eli paid her.

This bag will work anywhere in the world!

With Eli hugging the globe, they left the shop. Su and Em swung the bag between them.

Suddenly, Em stopped. "Hey, there's a label tied to the handle," she said. She read it out.

"How can a bag not work?" asked Su. They tried to undo the clasp but they couldn't.

"We don't need the bag," said Eli. But Em wouldn't give up. She pulled at the clasp so hard, she fell over.

Em fell on Su who fell on Eli. The globe crashed to the ground and broke in two. "Can we glue it?" said Em.

She held the halves together. As if by magic, the globe was whole again. They were amazed.

The key inside this cheer-up box. But you each country I visited,

Happy *Egbert*

This is a magical world with it and you are shown in my portrait. globe will take you to the

Dear Fellow Explorer,

globe opens my special will only reach it if you visit and collect all of my things.

exploring!
Boff

globe. I went all over the can too. The globe will take Look out for the things that When you find one, the next place.

"Look!" said Su. "Something's fallen out of the globe."

It was a piece of paper as thin as a butterfly's wing. As Su unfolded it, the paper fell apart and a key fell out.

Whatever could it open? Su put the letter together, to see if it told her.

Can you help her piece together the letter? What does it say?

On safari

"Exploring?" said Eli. He began to feel excited. "A special box? And all we have to do is find Egbert's things?" Em and Su's eyes lit up for a second.

"But the lady said he only pretended to explore," Su said. Eli looked at the globe again. Under his fingers, it was beginning to spin.

It spun faster and faster. The whole world became a whirling merry-go-round. Suddenly it stopped. Em, Su and Eli swayed where they stood, feeling dizzy.

They could hardly believe their eyes. The shop had vanished. "Isn't it hot," said Em. "What's happened?"

"Wow," said Su. "Maybe the globe *is* magic."

"A lion?" cried Eli. "RUN!"

They scrambled up a tree for safety. Eli gazed at all the animals around them. "We're in Africa," he said.

The lion ambled away. Eli started to climb down. He wanted a closer look at the zebras. But a twig caught his T-shirt. He wriggled, almost knocking a nest off its branch.

Then he saw something inside the nest. He recognized it at once from the painting of Egbert in the junk shop.

What has Eli spotted?

7

On top of the world

This looks like my poster of the Himalayas!

Eli grasped the telescope. None of them saw the globe begin to turn. It whirled them away.

They landed on a high mountain peak. "I wanted to explore Africa," Em moaned. "Where are we?"

Eli felt peculiar. He didn't like being so high. The globe fell from his hands. Su dived after it.

Too late. The three of them watched in horror as it bounced down a ravine.

As it fell, the globe spun. They spun too, landing on a path in front of a hut.

The globe was a long way down. It would be tricky, but they had to rescue it.

"Look what I've found," said Su. She held up a rope and two sturdy sticks. "We can use these to climb down, like hikers."

"But there are three of us," said Em. "We'll need another stick."

"I can see one," called Eli.

Leaning against some rocks, was a walking stick carved with the familiar letters EB. Eli gripped it and held on tight.

Su took the telescope. "The globe's trapped near a bridge. Hold the rope and follow me."

Can you find a safe way down?

9

Sun and sand

As Eli freed the globe, it spun. The mountains melted away and they fell through space.

They landed, *bump!* on scorching sand. The air was hot and dry. "We must be in a desert," said Su.

The bag burst open as it hit the sand. Three scarves trailed out. Em tugged one. "Let's put them on."

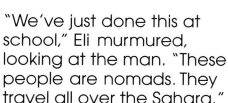

As they wound the scarves around them, a line of people and camels appeared. Quickly, they hid behind a bush.

A man in a white scarf put up his hand. The camels stopped. "This is good," the man said. "We shall make camp here."

"We've just done this at school," Eli murmured, looking at the man. "These people are nomads. They travel all over the Sahara."

A boy about Eli's age, carried a baby goat over to their bush. "Who are you?" he asked in surprise. "Were you separated from your tribe?"

Before they could answer, a man shouted, "Akhaya!" The boy turned. "It's my job to fetch the water," he told them. Where from? Em wondered.

The boy rode a camel with a rope tied to its saddle. As he rode away, a bag of water rose out of the ground. It was a well in the middle of the desert.

Su licked her dry lips. "I've never felt so thirsty in my life," she whispered. A smell of cooking filled the air. Eli's tummy rumbled.

The boy from the camel spoke to the man in the white scarf. Then he waved the three over. "Come, my father says eat with us."

As they walked to the tents, Eli grabbed Su's arm in excitement. "I can see something of Egbert's," he said.

Can you?

11

A wide, dark river

Eli was given the spoon. Now they had three things in the bag. Where would the globe go next?

It grew hot and damp. Branches above them hid the sky. The air was full of buzzing and humming.

They were on a river bank. Eli nearly fell in. "Look out, there might be crocodiles," said Su.

A large can poked out of the bag. Su shook it and sprayed it all over them.

"Yeuch! That's disgusting," Eli spluttered. "It smells like rotting hamburgers."

Em pointed to a huge, spotty flower. "The smell's coming from that."

"Squark!" said a voice and they jumped. A suspicious parrot had fixed two beady eyes on them.

Su saw a gliding tree frog. "They really glide," she said. "And suckers on their toes stick to the trees."

"Hey," said Em, waving the telescope at a tree. "I can see Egbert's helmet. It's been used as a nest."

Su was the best climber so she went to get it. Vines hung down around her. She used them to climb up the trunk.

Em watched Su go higher. Then, to her amazement, she saw a twig begin to crawl. It was a stick insect.

Em and Eli looked more closely. Lots of creatures were cleverly disguised, to merge into the jungle around them.

I've just seen a snake and a moth.

I can see a chameleon and a turtle.

"Got it," Su called, clutching the helmet. All of a sudden, she looked terrified. "This tree is dangerous. Come on globe. Spin NOW!"

Can you spot the creatures they saw? Do you know what scared Su?

Monkey mischief

"That was a narrow escape," said Em. "Where are we now?" They stood in a hot, noisy, busy street.

Su smiled. "I know," she said. "My Gran's told me so much about it – India."

A boy rushed past them, carrying a carpet. "It's the same as Egbert's scarf in the picture," cried Em. "Let's follow him."

The boy paused to talk to the driver of a little yellow cab. Then he vanished down a side street. "We'll never find him now," Su panted.

But the driver heard her. "The boy is my cousin," he told them. "He works at the Carpet Emporium, most beautiful of all carpet makers. Would you like a lift?"

The second they climbed aboard, they were off. The driver sped along, not stopping for anyone. It was a very bumpy ride.

At last, he stopped outside a low, white house. A man with a big smile welcomed them. "Hello! You wish to buy a carpet, no?"

"Er, no," said Su. She pointed to a half-made carpet. "We're looking for a scarf with that pattern. It's quite old."

14

"This dirty old rag?" said the man, holding out a scarf. "No, we'll make you a fine, new one."

"We *really* like that one," said Su. The man was baffled. He shrugged and gave it to them.

Outside, disaster struck. A monkey snatched the scarf. "Hey, we need that," Eli yelled, giving chase.

The monkey scampered down the street. Soon he was lost in the turmoil of people and animals.

"I can't see him anywhere," Eli said sadly. Su couldn't see him either. Just then, Em spotted him.

Where is the monkey?

The island in the lake

Em threw some nuts to the monkey. Su took the scarf. The globe turned . . .

. . . and they were on an island. The sun shone brightly but it felt very cold.

Then the bag sprang open. Inside were pullovers and woolly hats with ear flaps.

They were pulling the clothes on when a boy walked up to them.

"Hello," said the boy. "Did you come over with the floating market?"

Eli looked blank. Where were they? They went from place to place so quickly.

A girl tugged the boy's sleeve. "Sergio, we must go or we'll miss the race. They've already started building the boats."

"OK Luisa," the boy smiled. "Today's the Lake Titicaca boat race," he explained. "Our father builds the best reed boats in all Bolivia!"

On the shore, people were twisting thick bundles of reeds. Eli, Em and Su watched astounded, as the boats took shape.

Soon the first boat was ready. "My father's," said the boy proudly.

But as his father was launching the boat, he tripped and hurt his arm.

Now he couldn't row. The boy's face fell. His father had worked so quickly. But he had lost before the race had even started.

"I'll row," Em cried. She seized the oar and was off. Em rowed frantically. A second boat was right on her tail.

Em rowed faster still. She shot past the finish. She'd won. The boy's father was thrilled. "The prize is yours," he said. "You earned it."

As Em took her prize, the globe began to spin. "Why did you do it?" Eli asked her.

Do you know why?

Children's Day

The globe whizzed around. Towering skyscrapers loomed over them. Then POP!

They were in a crowded park. As she landed, Em burst a boy's balloon. He cried out in surprise.

"Sorry," said Em. "I didn't see you. Where are we?"

The boy was bewildered. "In Japan, of course," he said. He bowed. "My name is Takashi. Who are you?" Su told him. She wondered if she should bow too.

"Where did you come from?" Takashi asked. Eli looked at the others and then the globe. Should he explain about Egbert? Su and Em nodded. The whole story came out.

"I know of Explorer Boff," said Takashi. The others were startled. How could he know about Egbert?

"If you come to tea to celebrate Children's Day, my father can tell you all about him," Takashi said.

A giant cloth fish hung outside his house. Puffed up with wind, it looked as if it was swimming in the air.

Inside, they sat around a low table. Noodles sizzled and spat on a hot plate. But Eli couldn't use his chopsticks. "It takes practice," said Takashi.

"Mr. Boff met my grandfather," Takashi's father told them. "Mr. Boff gave him a box as a gift. My grandfather planted a tree in it. Please take it."

What could they give him? Su thought back. When they'd put on the pullovers, she'd seen the very thing.

Did you spot it too?

A red rock and a thirsty frog

As Takashi untied the ribbon on the box, the globe whisked them away. They were somewhere very hot with strange trees.

A kangaroo bounded past. Then they saw two koalas in a tree. There was no mistaking where they were now – Australia.

Three hats flew out of the bag. Em caught one. At the same time, Su spotted a boomerang behind a bush.

I bet it's the biggest rock in the world!

But as she went to pick it up, the globe spun. "Hey, stop! We've only just arrived," cried Eli. His voice was drowned out by a loud booming.

"Wanna go inside the rock?" asked a man in red shorts. Eli, Em and Su followed a family of tourists into the cave.

Can you guess how the rock came to be here? Once upon a time, it was a frog! The biggest frog in the world. And this desert was its ocean.

All day long, the frog caught flies and swam. At night he slept on a lily pad. Until, one day, he woke up feeling very thirsty.

He drank and drank until he had emptied the ocean. There wasn't a drop of water left. And that's why there's only sand here today.

The man began to tell them a story in a sing-song voice. When the story ended, the tourists trailed out of the cave.

But Em had spotted something in a gap between the rocks. She went closer to investigate. A book was poking out.

Its pages crackled as Em picked it up. The book looked old and dirty and there was a strange label on the front cover.

At first, the label didn't make sense. Then Em realized it was in code. As she read it, the globe began to spin.

What does the label say?

YM YRAID YB TREBGE FFOB

21

Finding the way

Trees whirled around them. They were back in a forest. But it wasn't as damp as the Amazon.

Eli was holding the bag. All of a sudden, it sprang open. A note from Egbert flew out. It said he had left his compass behind in a house in the forest, and told them how to find it.

Can you find the house where Egbert left his compass?

Windmills and tulips

The compass was hanging from a tree outside the house. The globe turned and they were off again.

"Wow," cried Su. They had landed on bikes, which somehow seemed to know where to go.

Alongside them, windmills were pumping water. "This is Holland," said Em. "My cousin came here."

One of the windmills had a balcony. People were looking out. "Maybe we can climb up too," Su said.

There were lots of tourists. Leaving their bikes at the door, they went in. Ladders led up to different platforms. One by one, they panted to the top.

Eli took out Egbert's telescope. "There aren't any hills," he said in surprise. At that moment, without warning, a breeze lifted one of the windmill's arms.

The bag was hooked up by a handle. It swung into the air and hovered over them, almost out of reach. Su leapt to the rescue and only just caught it.

Feeling very relieved, they went back inside. A man was telling the visitors all about windmills.

"Millers sent each other messages by putting a windmill's arms in a certain position. They tied the sails on in different ways too."

Em had found a leaflet which showed some of the messages. She read it out to the others.

Some mills are used to grind corn. This one used to pump water. Now it's just for tourists!

VERTICAL SHAFT

CROWN WHEEL

PIT WHEEL

TAKE A PAIR HOME!

WINDMILL   MESSAGES

LOOK   OUT   ALL'S WELL   HELP

ON   IN   PIT WHEEL   CROWN WHEEL

Eli looked out of a window and saw a line of mills in the distance. "Hey," he said. "I think they have a message for us."

What does the message say?

Snowballs and surprises

There on the wheel were Egbert's clogs. Su picked them up. They were off.

But the globe stopped and they were left adrift. "It's stuck," Eli cried in a panic.

A chill wind blew around them. "Are there coats in the bag?" Su shivered.

Delving down, they found padded clothes, goggles and boots. When they were well wrapped up, the globe spun once more.

They landed somewhere cold and glistening white. Gulls screeched and slid on icebergs. Seals honked and flapped their flippers.

"This must be the North Pole," cried Em. "It's completely made of ice floating on the sea. There's no land at all."

Su wondered where the penguins were. "That's the South Pole," said Eli.

Em saw a hole in the ice and three rods. "Look, we can fish through the ice."

"I've got a bite," cried Su. But she didn't have a fish on the end of her line.

Just then, they heard loud creaking and cracking noises.

Eli smiled. "I remember reading about this," he said. "The ice makes those noises as it moves."

"But what's the hump over there?" Su asked. "A polar bear?" They crept up on it silently. It didn't move.

"It's an igloo," said Em, "A shelter made of snow. They're used by people on hunting trips."

"This is great," said Eli. "The globe isn't in such a hurry for once."

"Maybe it's frozen," said Su.

Why do you think the globe hasn't spun yet?

Journey's end

Em picked up Egbert's sock and the globe spun faster than ever. When it stopped, they were on the beach of a tropical island. A cross had been drawn in the sand.

"The cheer-up box!" cried Eli. It had been such an exciting day, they'd almost forgotten the key in the globe. Beside the sandy cross were three spades. Eli, Em and Su began to dig.

At long last, Em's spade hit something hard. She threw down the spade. Then she used her hands to scrape the sand away.

Carefully, Em lifted a small, wooden box out of the hole. Su fished for the key in her pocket. She put it in the lock and turned . . .

. . . click! The box flew open. Inside was a scrap of paper. "Still feeling fed-up?" it read. Eli laughed. "No," he said.

In a blink of an eye they were back home.

"Let's take Egbert's things to the lady in the shop," said Em. "We can tell her that he *was* an explorer after all."

Su looked inside the bag. "They're not here," she cried. Eli took the bag and turned it upside down. Souvenirs they had been given or found along the way fell out. But all of Egbert's things had gone.

"Maybe it's so someone else can find them," said Eli. "Come on, let's take back the globe and bag."

Before they do, look back. Can you spot where each souvenir came from?

Around the world

Back at the mall, they were amazed. Barely ten minutes had passed. Moments later, Aunt Rose arrived, very surprised at their sudden interest in geography.

She bought them a World Encyclopedia, for waiting so patiently. They found out lots more about the places they'd seen. Here is a page from their scrapbook.

Water lilies on the Amazon river can grow to over 1m (1.094 yds) in diameter. The smelly plant is called a rafflesia.

The tree we climbed in Africa is called a Baobab. It takes up lots of water when it rains and stores it in its trunk. That's why it always looks so fat.

In India, cows are sacred. They wander all over the street and the traffic has to go around them.

Ayers Rock in Australia belongs to the Aborigines, the first people to live in Australia. They call it Uluru. It is 600 million years old.

The fox at the North Pole was an Arctic fox. It's like European ones, but its coat is white. This makes it harder to see in the snow.

Bolivia is in South America. The lake we saw is the highest in the world that's big enough to sail on.

The fish hanging outside Takashi's house was a carp. In Japan, it means strength and determination.

さかな

Holland is part of the Netherlands. Years ago, people there wore wooden shoes called clogs. Now they are mostly made for visitors.

Answers

pages 2-3
The junk shop

The bag is by Eli's foot. It has been circled in this picture.

pages 4-5
Egbert the explorer?

When the letter is put together, it says:

Dear Fellow Explorer,

This is a magical globe. I went all over the world with it and you can too. The globe will take you everywhere I went. Look out for the things that are shown in my portrait. When you find one, the globe will take you to the next place.

The key inside this globe opens my special cheer-up box. But you will only reach it if you visit each country I visited, and collect all of my things.

Happy exploring!
Egbert Boff

pages 6-7
On safari

Eli has spotted Egbert's telescope. Here you can see it in the nest.

pages 8-9
On top of the world

The safe way to the globe is shown in red.

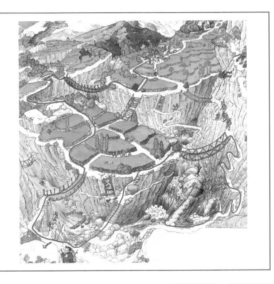

pages 10-11
Sun and sand

Eli saw Egbert's spoon. It is circled in the picture below.

pages 12-13
A wide, dark river

Su saw a jaguar in the tree. It is circled here, with the other creatures Em and Eli spotted.

snake   moth

jaguar

chameleon

turtle

pages 14-15
Monkey mischief

The monkey has climbed up a lamppost. You can see it circled below.

pages 16-17
The island in the lake

Em rowed because she had seen the prize – Egbert's hunting knife. It is circled below.

pages 18-19
Children's Day

Look back to page 16. In the bag with the pullovers is a gift-wrapped present.

pages 20-21
A red rock and a thirsty frog

Each word has been written back to front. The label reads:

MY DIARY
BY
EGBERT
BOFF

pages 22-23 Finding the way

Their way through the forest is shown in red.

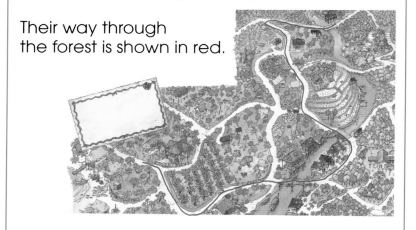

pages 24-25
Windmills and tulips

The message in the sails is: *Look on crown wheel.*

pages 26-27
Snowballs and surprises

The globe hasn't spun, because they haven't found anything of Egbert's yet. This arctic fox has one of his socks.

pages 28-29 Journey's end

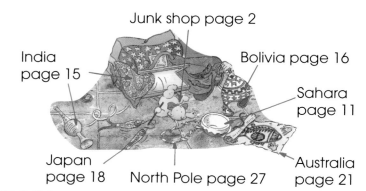

Junk shop page 2

India page 15

Bolivia page 16

Sahara page 11

Japan page 18

North Pole page 27

Australia page 21

page 4
The painting of Egbert

1. Telescope
2. Spoon
3. Clogs
4. Helmet
5. Scarf
6. Hunting knife
7. Collecting box
8. Walking stick
9. Sock

This edition first published in 2003 by Usborne Publishing Ltd., Usborne House, 83-85 Saffron Hill, London EC1N 8RT, England.

www.usborne.com Copyright © 2003, 1997 Usborne Publishing Ltd.

U.E. Printed in Portugal. First published in America March 1998.